Navigating Change

Navigating Change

The Quick Guide

Cameron C. Duncan

Published by Tablo

Table of Contents

Dedications

During the writing of this book on change, I have been undergoing a transformation of my own. I reflect on the people in my life who have taught me and inspired me to change, yet encouraged me to be authentic and unapologetic with who I am. We are people with flaws, passions, priorities, insecurities, and abilities. We are doing our best to get through this thing called life. I thank those of you who never stopped believing in me and never gave up on me.

Dedicated to the memory of my dear friend Kelly Rutt; you reminded me that friendship will not be absent of disagreement, but the power of our friendship will always be bigger than any disagreement. We must dare to be vulnerable to find our strength and we must lead with empathy to be transformative. Rest in Paradise.

To Rocky, Thank you for being my Rock and showing me unconditional love. We found each other when you were abandoned but it was you who rescued me. We both knew what it was like to be given up on, but we never gave up on each other. You never let the hard times that preceded our paths crossing define you. You just wanted everyone to be OK. Even as your body faded, your will and spirit were strong. You were funny, stubborn, gentle, and charming. I am sorry that I always made you get down from the couch. Rest in Paradise.

Special Thanks

Special thanks to Mom, and my sisters Connie and Sidney for checking on me. Thanks to my friend Amy for taking care of Rocky. Thanks to Ranya for being inspirational and keeping me sane this year. Thanks to Reina for feedback and suggestions. Thanks to Dad for encouraging me to jump years ago. Thanks to all of you who read this with an open mind on how to look differently at change.

Prologue

When I was 11 years old, before leaving basketball practice on a Wednesday evening, I was told by my coach that we had practice Saturday morning at 8am. My mother was a single parent who worked 60 hours a week running a hair salon. Unlike most of my teammates' parents she worked on Saturday mornings. I knew this change would be a problem that would require a disruption to her Saturday routine and schedule. I dreaded telling her because I felt she would be frustrated and angry. So instead of letting her know at once when she picked me up, which would have given her notice to plan on the best way to get me to practice that day, I waited until 7:15 Saturday morning, while she was putting on her make-up. You can imagine how angry she was. My intentions were good but my strategy and execution for managing this minor change was awful. I made it to practice that morning, but it was a quiet and uncomfortable ride. Additionally, I can imagine she arrived at work that day in a sour mood.

Fast forward decades later: I now grow more hair in my ears than on my head, my basketball dreams are over, and I have worked with multi-billion-dollar organizations and brilliant executives who have made the same mistake as that 8-year-old kid leading change in their organizations. Change is hard. Change is often the hardest thing we must do, plan for, communicate, and sustain. In this book I am going to help you become a better change navigator in your personal life and organization. My hope is that, as you turn these pages, you will gain perspectives, insights, and have a little fun in the process. I assure you this will not be like the textbooks that require Monster energy drinks to get through.

I will walk you through a new way of thinking about change management: as change navigation. I'll explain what I mean by change navigation, so that you can start leading your team or organization more effectively. You'll learn exactly why people have the responses they do to change, and how to best anticipate and respond to their concerns. I'll also bust some common myths and jargon in change management, so you can get down to what matters most: people's experience of change. Are you ready to think more like a captain and less like a manager? Let's get started.

What's Your Why?

The influential speaker Simon Sinek suggests that when you are trying to influence people to believe in your product or vision, you should start with *Why*. I absolutely agree; everything we are motivated to do in life has a *why* behind it, from the most mundane to the most exceptional undertakings and challenges we accept. Let's start with why are you reading this? Did someone you trust or respect recommend this to you? Do you aspire to be a better leader of change? Do you just want to expand your knowledge base? Behind your *why* that came to mind, there is a deeper *why*. For example, you admire and respect lots of people that recommend books to you, but you never read them all. What is special about your relationship with this person? Why is it important for you to be a better change leader or change ambassador? Why do you crave knowledge? Our true *why* is not typically what we articulate or think of at first.

We communicate the why in the shallowest of explanations which do not really explain the why's that have become ingrained in our subconscious as our motivators. Your why is the foundation on which your personal and work life is built. Your why's are not always so different than your peers. You may go to work because you believe in the purpose behind what you do, but you also go to work to survive, provide, and live a life with the ability to afford comforts and experiences. What are your life's ambitions? Are any of them related to getting promotions or saving your company money? Is anything on your bucket list about being more efficient? If you say yes, then you need to read an entirely different book called the *Art of Happiness* by the Dalai Lama. But most of us have a powerful why that skilled salesmen and politicians know how to tap into to earn your votes and dollars. However, organizationally, people can have little understanding or connection to the why of the change presented to them. So why do project teams spend so much time building boring and empty Why's? The answer is perspective. Most projects go through the process of intake, which includes a project charter scope, and business case. This is not a Project Management course so I will not go into detail on these documents but if they are foreign to you, Google them. The beginning of the project process is largely tied to getting approval for funding and resourcing by senior management. As a result, the preparation and analysis of value is catered to the perspective of senior leadership which is less than 1% of your audience population.

Change navigation cannot just be about appeasing or placating leadership. You need to identify and connect with the other 99%. Think about the reason people should go on this journey with you. Think of the why as the foundational building block for any change. Would you build a house on mud? Would you build it with sticks or straw? If your foundation is shaky, anything you build is susceptible to collapse when the climate changes. However, if your foundation is strong, it will be more stable amid the chaos that change can create. Start with why: why does your organization need this, and why do the people being asked to change need this? What is your why to be a navigator? Now that you have a why, let's go to what.

What is it?

One of the reasons I decided to write this book is because, over the years, I have grown rather tired of how Change Management has become an industry buzzword. The phrase change management is often used in reference to change control as well. What I realized is that the problem is not how people misuse the words change management; the problem is that we have incorrectly termed what we do as change practitioners as Change Management. But before we go into why change management as a term doesn't actually fit, let's talk about what Change Management is as it's currently understood.

Change Management, defined by the ACMP (Association of Change Management Professionals), is the practice of applying a structured approach to the transition of an organization from a now state to a future state to realize expected value through focusing on the "People Side of Change." That means helping people be successful with change so you can reach your desired goals or outcomes. By the way, the ACMP is to Change Managers what PMP is to Project Managers.

So, what isn't change management?

First, **change management is not** the same as Change Control. This term is often incorrectly referred to as being interchangeable with Change Management.

To clarify this difference, I prefer the term "Change Navigation," because your essence as a change leader is to help people successfully reach the desired destination at the end of their change journey.

Change Management is **not a communication plan**. However, a communication plan is an important part of Change Navigation. A communication plan helps communicate and execute the integral aspects of your change strategy. If you thought sending an email before Go Live was "Change Management," I'm very glad you're reading this.

When you create your communication plan, you need to first understand and plan what you need to communicate. You need to discover what people want to know, who needs to know, when they need to know it, and how you can reach them. If you don't, your communication plan might as well be junk mail.

Think about it this way, if you went to a nutritionist for a nutrition plan, they wouldn't just give you a plan blindly. They would learn about your diet goals, your allergies, your preferences to be more energetic, lose weight, gain weight, any religious dietary restrictions, etc.

But after all that, is a nutrition plan enough to change your diet or your body? You need motivation to stick with the plan, you need to know how to prepare the meals, how to train your body, how to get back in the saddle when you've eaten too many Doritos. That is Change Navigation, because you need help to get to the destination on your journey of change.

Finally, change management **isn't project management**. This is not a jab at the valuable profession of project management, it's just we have a particular set of skills and perspective, or at least we should!

The main difference between these two professions is the core focus, People. The Change Manager or Practitioner is focused on the people first; Project Managers are focused on the tasks. The Change Manager makes sure the people are successful at adopting the change, so it happens effectively. For example, a Project Manager wants to make sure training is completed on time, and on budget. The Change Manager's goal is to make sure that people have the knowledge they need to be successful. Project Managers and Change Managers should be partners in change; we need each other. If you are Project Manager being tasked to be the Change Manager also, you will need to learn how to set your PM hate down and think more about people's needs for success.

From the Change Management perspective, you may often need to slow down the project plan to make sure that people are ready to move forward. Using the above example, a project manager may be concerned that project training is behind schedule and want to reduce the duration to make up time. Whereas the Change Manager may request to extend the training timelines or activities because training has not been effective enough in equipping people with the knowledge and skill level to change. Project Managers may also want less activities to reduce costs, time, and effort but Change Managers understand the Return on investment of a strong comprehensive change strategy.

The Project Manager is also traditionally focused on the project team, the Change Manager is out among the people, across all organizational roles, gathering information and insights. If you think the role of a change professional is all C-suites and board rooms, you are overlooking the true nature of the role. This is a role of the people and as you navigate change you should be out among the people often. The change strategy should be translated into activities to be added to a project plan where applicable. I say where applicable because not all change efforts are projects. In fact, most change efforts are not projects. However, the profession has largely become associated with projects such as Technology implementations. There is more to change such as transforming employee morale, mergers, restructuring, working remotely during a pandemic, and so on. These types of changes don't typically have project plans because they are so uniquely different.

For example, if we had the challenge to change the mindset in which floor supervisors lead assembly line workers because coercive management styles were damaging employee relations and morale, that is not something you can just project manage to resolve.

Now that you know what Change Management is, what will it take to be a true Change Navigator?

It will require a will to put people first even when it is not convenient to do so and commitment to support people's success in change.

Too often people talk about change management in terms of overcoming resistance to change, or as just managing people through a new process. When you google Change Management, you will find numerous articles on "Managing Change." I contest that it is our not our role to *manage change*, because it is natural and instinctual for people to hate change. To manage implies that we are controlling that reaction. We have little control over how people react to and perceive change, but we can help navigate them through the process of change, by providing them with what they need to join us on our change journey. We can then make their change experience as positive as possible and generate excitement for the future. But to get to that point we need to visualize, empathize, strategize, and energize on the best way forward. I encourage you to think of change as a destination: Where are you going? Why are you going? And how are you going to get there? What are the obstacles? What kind of experience do you want to provide?

What is Change Navigation?

Change Navigation is the process of leading people safely and successfully through the stages of the human change journey to their new desired state or opportunity. Safely! Why is safety important? You want people to feel secure in the way they operate and communicate in the future. If you are leading change as an employee, the people you navigate through change once will travel with you again. When people are confident that you are reliable and dependable to get them where they need to go in change, it will benefit you in the long term. What makes change navigation so different from change management? Perspective. The word *management* can imply controlling tasks or regulation.

As mentioned previously, change management is often used interchangeably with compliance requirements for change control. Navigation means to figure out a course and travel a distance. As a change navigator people will need your help to find the best course to get them to the future. Your journey may be faced with a variety of obstacles, challenges, and options. It is important to embrace a mindset that allows you to be versatile, prescriptive, and open to new ideas and methods of navigating. In my 15 years of experience leading change, I have earned a few gray hairs in my beard, but my greatest challenge has not been the people affected by change but rather the people leading the change. Seems a little strange right? Not really because people affected by change tend to be self-aware that they are struggling with change and they can provide the reasons why, which provides me something to work with and strategize-- therefore less gray hair.

People leading or captaining the change often see resistance as a burden and place the responsibility of change on the passengers. This is because they are focused on managing change rather than navigating it. A major reason for this mindset is the why. Why is a change management effort important? If the why is related to project success or leadership outcomes, the people's resistance to change becomes an inconvenience or burden to those goals. Your why should be truly meaningful for the audience. The hard truth about change management and the reason why it can be thought of as a buzzword is because the out of the box approach is a plug and play, one size fits all change strategy. Unfortunately, it is more common than I'd like to believe. Consulting firms often want to be efficient by transferring the same change strategies from one client to the next. I aim to challenge this approach. Navigating people is not subject to a simple blueprint like building a house or manufacturing a product. People are dynamic; they have unique needs, priorities, and are susceptible to extraneous variables such as fatigue, environment, and organizational blocks. I have seen consultants share their change management strategies for a new initiative, using a presentation slide that references the previous company. I get it, it's easier to plug and play than start from scratch and is great to have a methodology or framework, but your plan needs to be tailored to your current journey. The flight plan to New York should not be the same as the flight plan to Paris, even though you are using the same pilot, staff, plane, and instruments.

In addition to the plug and play method, The check box approach is another flawed Change method. This approach occurs when the change leaders see navigating change as nothing more than a tool to get people to buy in. Under this approach the change team or project team focus simply on completing a change in management activity or task like training or sending a communication. As change navigators your focus is not on completing a task but to accomplish your purpose. Why is that important? Completing training as a task does not mean people have gained knowledge competency or are comfortable in the new way of working. It just means they sat through training. Sending a communication just means a message was sent but does not ensure that it was received, deciphered, and understood the way it was intended. If we focus on what we are trying to accomplish rather than a task, we can strategize much more effectively. Let's make this personal: suppose you want someone to marry you, or you want to be convinced to marry someone. Most would agree that dating is a key step in that process. Could you assume that because you completed a date or two that you are ready for a marriage? A lot goes into that right? To date effectively, you need to establish a purpose of what you want the dating outcome to be, and you should plan the date to allow you to reach that that outcome. I personally never understand why people would go to the movies on a first date because the objective is to get to know someone, so you can assess if there will even be another date. I hope that makes sense because I am a much better change leader than dater. We don't live to complete tasks, we complete tasks to point us towards the outcomes we want.

Unfortunately, sometimes the intent of the change management plan by people who are not skilled in change is to just complete a change management plan so if things don't work, they can say to their leadership, "Hey, we had a change management plan and it still didn't work." As a change navigator your goal is to support and lead people through the journey of change. Your change strategy should be designed to address how you can make people be successful in change. This will often require creative solutions. This is not to suggest that the different methodologies of change you may have learned such as ADKAR or Kotter are without merit or value. In this book we will focus on outcomes over task and how to align our perspective and strategy to meet those outcomes. My ask of you is that you let go of the check box approach of thinking of change as a task rather than a purpose.

Back to change navigation: think about what the outcome of your activity is and strategize toward that. For example, the object of training is knowledge development. From a communication aspect, what do you want the audience to understand and how do you want to them feel about the message? Is this the information they need to know?

Like navigators on their first boat, I have an OAR for you; these will help you to plan your journey and not get stuck on just completing tasks.

Outcomes-What outcomes do you want to achieve with this activity?

Assessment-How will you assess whether your outcomes were reached?

Results-What did the results of your assessment tell you? Are you ready to move forward or do we need to do more work at this stage?

Now Oar you ready to move on?

Why do people need navigators?

People fear change, they fear uncertainty, they fear the unknown. People need security, assurance, and guidance

Think about your daily routine, or your daily commute. You can do so many things in your life almost on autopilot. When you start something new and disrupt that routine, you create the need for your brain to spend a lot of extra energy. Adopting a new behavior, even a modest one, takes work and replication.

For example, have you ever needed to make a stop at the store after work and then got home and realized you completely forgot? Or maybe you caught yourself driving to your old job after you started a new one. Don't worry, you're not just losing your mind!

Your brain perceives change the same way it does fear, resulting in a Fight or Flight response. Yes, the same flight or flight reaction you may experience when suddenly spotting a cougar on your normal leisurely Sunday hike. Having a strong reaction to change is natural. After this section you'll be able to understand the role that fear plays in navigating change, and how to work your team through it.

Fear and anxiety are often categorized as resistance. People frequently use the phrase "managing resistance" when they talk about change, but that has negative connotations. It doesn't set you up to navigate change well. When you think of people as resistors it can put the onus on them being the problem that needs to be managed. The truth is we are generating the problem that they are reacting to and so it is your responsibility to support them. Your role is to help people move forward, not control people from resisting. If you understand change is natural, you can focus on how to proactively address people barriers to change.

One of the most important ways to help people navigate change is by communicating. When you're uncertain, your brain craves information, so you rely on past experiences or create stories to fill that void. Unfortunately, people are very bad at guessing and will often assume the worst. People would rather conclude that they're all getting laid off or doomed to fail rather than not know. When leading change, you must prepare for that impulse and get ahead of it.

There is an OLD G.I.J.O.E saying that "now you know and knowing is half the battle." That couldn't be truer in navigating change. So, when you're leading change, share as much information as you can, early and often. Monitor the rumor mills and make sure to address any misinformation that may be circulated.

Develop a cadence for communication. That way people don't just hear from you at the beginning; you shouldn't just dump a ton of information on them and then leave them in the dark. When you communicate, deliver meaningful information. If you are constantly communicating the same or generic info, you will lose the attention of your audience and they may start to ignore you.

Finally, create platforms for two-way communication. Don't just inform; give them a chance to respond, and keep an open dialogue. This is important to build trust and gain new information about challenges you may not have expected. You may even learn that there are adjustments needed to make the solution or destination more attractive.

Now, I already hear you asking: What if the change is confidential? Even in that case, share what you can, as much as you can and let people know when you will be able to share more.

As I mentioned earlier if you don't give people information, they'll start filling in the blanks themselves with the worst possible outcomes so hiding info doesn't reduce fear; it increases it.

You now know that change is natural, and that people need information to get through the process of change. When you're successful in communicating, the possibilities are endless.

Navigating Change Myths

Myth or Fact: The definition of insanity is doing the same thing over and over expecting different results.

The answer is Myth: the definition of insanity is extreme folly or unreasonableness or a severely disordered state of mind.

What you may know to be the definition of insanity is an Albert Einstein quote, and he wasn't even a psychologist!

There are common myths about Change Management too.

Let's bust 3 of them:

Myth 1: People don't have a choice- This couldn't be further from the truth. People have a choice, even if you take away the current state such as technology or software. People do not have to follow the new way or adopt new behaviors in a manner that will yield successful results. For example, at what percentage level of your capability do you need to run at to keep your employment in good standing? And if you say 100% this means that you need 7-8 hours of sleep, every night, no distractions, no illness, no physical, mental, or spatial limitations to be effective. In short, a near impossibility. What if I told you on average people are only productive for about 3 hours a day? Just for the sake of Math let's say you can do your job competently at about 40% of your capability. But happy employees give 55% effort by choice. People always have a choice on what effort level they give their role without being at risk of losing it. This matters because organizational success and productivity relies on the contributions of individuals and groups; forcing adoption of a new behavior does not ensure that behavior will yield the desired benefits. In fact, it could have a negative impact on the organization.

People can also leave the organization.

The long-term impacts of this philosophy are problematic; in some cases you may get people to follow orders to comply, but each time you do this, you lose trust, and you create a negative connection with future changes. This can make future change more difficult. Conversely, if you focus on navigating people through change, you'll find that when a change needs to be implemented quickly, you can leverage earned trust to help move challenging change forward.

Think about a time you worked a little late to help a good colleague or gave up your Saturday plans to help a friend move. You have a why! You care about your relationship with that person, you trust their intentions and you want them to succeed. If you're genuine in helping others, they will help you too.

Myth 2: They don't need to know-Today's workforce is highly intelligent, educated, and resourceful. A common myth in change is that many people heavily impacted by the change don't need to know about the change until it happens.

This is a wonderful way to fail. Keeping people in the dark can have disastrous consequences in providing the right solutions, understanding the gravity of impacts, and preparing people. You may not want to bother them yet, but delaying information can cause people to rebel or refuse change when you are ready to launch. Some things are confidential, and you may have concerns about creating havoc by letting the cat out of the bag before you are ready. But provide information where you can and let people know when they can expect more information.

Myth 3: It's not a big deal- Change efforts have a tendency to be underestimated. This is because the people proposing the change may not understand the gravity and details of the change impacts for people. Project Managers may assume that the change management component is not necessary.

Assess each change by evaluating who's going to be impacted and how. Analyze the complexity of change from the perspectives of those with intimate knowledge of the current vs future state. Place your team in the best position to succeed by ensuring you have the right level of change support. It's better to overestimate the change efforts needed and adjust later than to underestimate and then try to upscale.

So next time you think about change, remember these **truths** of change management:

Truth #1: People always have a choice

Truth #2: People do need to know

Truth #3: Don't gamble that it's not a big deal - it is.

Truth #4: Just because someone quoted it, doesn't mean it's true.

Write these down somewhere you can keep track of them, and you'll be well on your way to navigating change better.

Preparing for departure

Would you buy a travel package with no destination? What if it was all expenses paid? One percent of the people reading this would. The other 99% would not. I am part of that 99%. I am adventurous at times, but not that adventurous. The point of any journey is the destination; if the destination does not align with our vision or provide value to us it is not worth the expense. Well, what if it's free? A free journey does not exist because any journey requires your most valuable asset. Any guesses of what that is?. The answer is Time. If you are a college student reading this, you may not yet fully understand the value of time because you have an abundance of it. However, as you advance in life and your career, you will learn how time becomes an invaluable resource. It is why you have less friendships as you get older and why you will pay for services you would have done yourself previously, like washing your car. If you are an experienced professional, you have an abundance of priorities that require the limited time you have; while you can always make more money you can never get back your time. Translating that back into your organization, you may think of change as free to your audience because they are not being asked to open their wallets, but every change takes up their time. Learning a new behavior or diverting their attention to learn about something new means they have less time to focus on other goals, and responsibilities. It is likely that you are not the only change navigator vying for their attention and buy-in. Think of this when you are communicating with your audience. What makes your change so special? How is your change worth the price of their time? Learn how you can reduce the price of changing and increase the value of your destination.

Where would you like to travel next? Picture the best part of your future excursion: what are you doing, how do you feel, who are you with? What if I told you that the captain or pilot in charge of getting you to your desired destination decided to skip the maintenance review, ignored the environmental conditions and potential weather hazards, didn't bother to turn on their radar, and the crew was scarce and unhelpful; would you reconsider? What if when you complained, the customer service agent insisted that you were overreacting because it's an easy trip? Does that journey sound inviting? No matter how much you desire to get where you are going, you would not be as excited about embarking on this expedition. You may be quite upset and demand a refund or another service provider.

Well, this happens constantly in change; often change leaders do not accurately assess change and most often the level of change effort needed to be successful is underestimated. People mean well, but it is just natural to underestimate what we don't know. Think of your own role in work or even your personal relationships. Do you think that others understand all of what you do? They may see the obvious things but it's only a fraction of what you actually do. Furthermore, your roles at work and in life have interactions which people who are not in your position may not be aware of. Take time to assess your change by involving the people who will be affected by it; it will help you to set up your change journey for success. Here is some TREAD to help you get traction when lifting off for change.

Time-How much time will a successful journey take?

Risk-What obstacles or challenges could derail your journey?

Environment-What environmental or organizational factors exist that you need to account for? For example, are you planning a restructure, weeks after one of your market peers laid off 1500 employees? Did your workforce recently complete a major change? These are environmental factors that could affect how people perceive and react to change.

Audience-Identify who will need to take part in this journey, and what their role is.

Difficulty-Research how challenging or complex this journey will be. Are you climbing Mt. Everest; are you changing minds and hearts? Difficult change takes time, resources, and energy.

When you do not assess the chance journey ahead, you are failing the people on this journey with you. You are putting the change effort at risk for failure and potentially damaging trust and culture. Conversely, by taking the time to prepare for your journey you can ensure that your initiatives have the time, resources, and information necessary to have smoother lift off and better passenger experience.

The Change Journey

Change as a Journey. Take 10 seconds and think about a major change that you made in your life.

How did you feel about it initially? Were you nervous, excited, fearful? What helped you decide to make the change?

Most likely you went through a process for change: your own change journey.

In this lesson, I'll walk you through a model of a change journey so that you can use it to guide your team through their next big change.

That journey may have looked like this. This is the Kubler-Ross change curve, and it gives us a model for thinking about the journey we all go on when we experience change.

The Kübler-Ross change curve

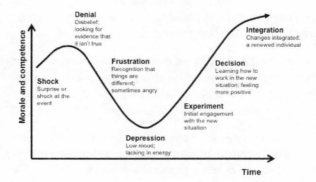

The first phase is the Shock phase: "I can't believe this is happening"

Then you move to Denial: "This isn't happening"

Next is Frustration, that feeling of: "I don't understand this"

Afterwards you may experience Grief: "I'm going to fail, I want to quit, I'm not capable"

Next is Experimentation: "Well maybe if I..." Now you're at the upswing of the change journey.

You then move to Decision to Integration: "Perhaps I can do this"

And finally, Integration and Excitement: "I'm doing it; I did it!"

You may notice that I skipped the Depression stage. That is the stage you want to avoid if possible. This is a point where people believe they are doomed to fail.

Not every journey is the same - you and the team you lead won't always follow this exact pattern. Sometimes you start at the beginning, and sometimes you start closer to the end for those changes you're excited about.

But it's important to understand this model because, as a leader of change, you need to be prepared to navigate your team through that journey, with its hills and valleys.

It's also important to understand that when you learn your team is going through these aspects of change, it's normal. You don't need to panic or be reactive. Instead, stay proactive in thinking: "This is where we are now, and how do we get to that next step?"

The Change Journey is not linear, and people can go backwards at times. The reasons for that could be miscommunication, rumors, uncertainty, or other factors like the loss of interest in the destination. Marriage is one of the biggest commitments and changes many people will incur in life. However, 20% of engagements end prior to marriage. This illustrates that, as people, no matter how excited and committed we think we are to the future state, we change our minds as new information emerges or our perception of the destination changes.

Your goal should be to keep the momentum going forward. You can do that by communicating often and effectively. That means listening intently and using the information you gain to build on or alter your approach to best support them.

Think of yourself as a Captain rather than a manager. Your goal is to get people safely to their destination. And remember: the power of your ship will be your Why.

Why should they embark upon this journey with you? Why should they trust you to captain that trip? Knowing your why and sharing it with your team is critical in getting you through those rocky waters.

Navigating with Empathy

"Walk a little in my shoes; see what I see, hear what I hear, feel what I feel, then maybe you will understand why I am the way I am."

I love this quote becomes it focuses on perspective. Without going into a psychology tangent, as people we are susceptible to unconscious bias, self-fulfilling prophecy, and confirmation bias that can distort our view of environments and our perceptions of others. You know your own abilities, challenges, priorities, and motives but that does not mean you know that of others. Each of us has entirely different experiences in life so it is impossible to always know what people need unless you are willing to listen.

The best way to gain another's perspective and be able to empathize is to walk in their shoes.

Be proactive in immersing yourself in the environment and experience of those impacted. As a change leader you need to make it your mission to gain insights and understanding of the different challenges people are facing. Ask questions and build relationships. Release yourself from the shackles of your desk and be among the passengers you are navigating. People need a captain not just a pen pal.

Find Change Agents and champions. Change Agents are critical to providing firsthand accounts of how change impacts their prospective areas and they can serve as critical liaisons to speak on behalf of the others passengers on your change journey.

Champions are trusted resources for communicating details of change, and they have the perspective of and empathy for their teams. Many people are most comfortable speaking with their change agents because they speak their language.

Your homework is to make time to connect with people throughout your organization to understand their challenges and goals as well as what they see as opportunities.

Build a strong network of Change Agents that represents the departments, roles, sites, regions, and countries of your organization.

When possible, instead of sending that email, stop by and have a conversation.

Empathy and perspective is also shown through our actions as well as our words. Avoiding buzzwords and jargon can help people understand you and allows you to connect with people at their level or language. So let's talk about it!

"Jargon" refers to those special words or expressions used by a particular profession or group that are difficult for others to understand.

If you're using these Jargon words, please reconsider.

Stakeholder

Who are you calling a stakeholder!

Every time I hear the word stakeholder, I hear my 9th grade teacher Mr. Lawrence scratching chalk against the blackboard to get the attention of my rowdy classmates, then I picture stake wielding villagers trying to save Wynona Ryder in Bram Stoker's *Dracula*. I never think of myself.

But I wondered if maybe I that needed to change the way I thought about "Stakeholders." Maybe I was being too critical, so I asked a colleague what Stakeholder meant to her. She replied, "It's like the important people like Directors and VP's." She was right--it was meant for important people, but important people aren't just Directors and VP's.

When you use the word "Stakeholders" when speaking to your audience, you may give them the impression that those "important people" are somehow different from them. I cannot count how many times I have seen a presentation inform an entire organization that key stakeholders were consulted in planning for the change. People could infer that if they weren't invited, they were not "key" or important.

Your words can disqualify your audience and, ultimately, encourage them to stop listening to you. Does that mean you can never use the word Stakeholder? No, but look at it this way...Who in your life outside of work do you refer to as a Stakeholder? Have you ever called a member of your family or friends "key stakeholders in the decisions you make"? No, so why do you use it?

Users- If you're at a tech company, this is probably a big one. This word just doesn't create any connection to what you're trying to do; it's very generic and non-specific. Alternatives could be SuperUser, as it gives people the feeling of expertise or wisdom. Experts or Customers are better words to use.

Scalable-What a building is to King Kong? I learned that it means able to grow. But I had to look it up, so chances are your audience may not know what this means either.

In the interest of time, we won't go through every jargon word, but the point is when navigating people through change, communicate and connect with people in a way they can understand, Jargon is easy but not effective. Be intentional, be clear, and project your empathy by using words that show people you are speaking the same language.

Change is good

Change can be a wonderful thing, I grew up in a time when all phones had cords and the length of that cord determined where you took the call. There was no online shopping, and we had to rewind the tape to replay the songs we liked. Thanks to Smartphones, imagine how much doctors' offices save on magazine subscriptions.

The ability to change and adapt to our environments is critical for our survival both personally and organizationally. Even the strongest organizations become obsolete and die if they don't change successfully. Maybe a certain video rental store comes to mind.

But change is challenging. People need help seeing the vision and opportunities that lie ahead of them, or even the doom they can prevent by changing. You can help them see those benefits by using a practice called **Tombstones and Lifelines**.

Tombstones and Lifelines are kind of like 'Pros and Cons.'

Tombstones are the dangers to you or your organization if you do not change.

Lifelines are the opportunities for success and vitality if you do change.

I know this seems extreme but, to get the attention of your audience, you may need to explain to them how they or the organization can or will fail if you do not move forward. And how you can thrive if you do.

To do this activity, get help from people who are knowledgeable about the change and its impacts, including people who are downstream of the change, not just leadership.

Then, gather the project and change team together to make your list.

First think of your Tombstones: what would happen if we don't change? Think of the immediate and eventual impacts and even the worst possible case scenarios.

Now analyze your list. Do any of these Tombstones scare you or your team? If not, try again.

Once you have a cemetery of tombstones, build your lifelines.

Think of all the wonderful benefits that could manifest from this change. Be specific!

For example, don't stop at cost savings: how much would the cost savings be and how would those savings be applied to your audience? What does this technology, software, or process mean to your mission, purpose, employees, or customers?

Once you're finished look at this list again; does anything resonate with you? If not try again because if you're not excited or committed your audience will not be either.

If you do this right, you'll build a clear picture and story of how the change benefits the organization and the people in it at all levels. Now you're ready to begin to replace their discomfort with change and hope for a better way forward that's clear, impactful, and attainable.

The Change Experience

The Change Experience

While writing this, something occurred to me: the movie *Titanic*. For the sake of being tangential, I won't lament how much I loathe that movie. But I considered that when you think of a journey, you may envision multiple vehicles to get there: car, train, plane, or cruise. Common modes of transportations have classes that create entirely different experiences for the passengers that are willing to pay more. So, does that happen in change? Yes, it does. Should it? To an extent. But let's talk about it.

The people that pay the most in change are the ones who are most affected by it. Those are the people that must learn a new behavior, technology, or process, or have the greatest disruption to their life. This may be a bit of a different approach to how you think of change investment. The people who are paying the most should have the best experience. They deserve the VIP treatment; they deserve the convenience, they deserve accommodations. Unfortunately, sometimes we want them to pay the highest price, then pick up the trash and carry their own luggage.

Making Change Meaningful

When I was a kid, I watched a show called the *A-Team*. In every episode, the *A-Team,* led by John Hannibal Smith, would face a new challenge, and for each of these challenges they would put together a plan to overcome whatever obstacles lay ahead and save the day. At the end, while basking in a gleeful moment of another job well done, John Smith would say, "I love it when a plan comes together." One challenge to change is making it meaningful through connection,

As you navigate change, the important things you need to consider are:

One, **why is the change important?** Two, **why - from the view of your audience - is the change important?** And contrary to widespread belief they are *not* the same.

You should always start by pondering why your organization is implementing or undergoing this change at this time. Certainly, they think they have a good reason, but think through if it's a good reason in your view. There are many roles, goals, and priorities in your organization. The C-Suite is thinking about how to keep the organization viable for the future or how to please shareholders. People on the front lines are focused on how they can be successful in their roles.

All of these "Why's" are important but people tend to focus only on the benefits to the leadership, rather than what's meaningful to everyone. Then, when people don't buy in to the generic statements about cost savings, or efficiency, the narrative is that they're being resistant. But the truth is that they haven't bought into your why.

To make change meaningful you need to break down and translate the high-level why into something that the people you're leading on your journey can relate to.

This step must happen before anything else in the change process.

Let's translate this to a family. A person may inform their children that they're moving because they received a higher paying job in another state. The why for the parent is financial growth, professional development, but what's important to the children may be being close to their friends, or that this is the only home they've ever known. A parent should make sure to find a way to explain why the move is happening that's meaningful to their children, so they can share in that excitement.

So, make your change meaningful by explaining what it means for the future of your organization and the people in it, and why it's the right solution.

Finally, connect the why of the change to your organizational mission. Bring your mission to life! Don't bury it in meaningless jargon. For example, the St. Jude Children's Hospital has a great purpose that employees are committed to. It is less meaningful to talk about streamlined processes and more meaningful to focus on how a particular change relates to treating and saving the lives of children.

And if you get stuck, go back to what this change means for you. Why is the "why" strong enough to motivate you to change? Making change meaningful for others comes much easier if you consider what would be meaningful to you if you were in their position.

Create your story for change; people love stories. Storytelling is an underutilized but very valuable skill for leading change. In my professional career, I have been puzzled by how some corporations think of Storytelling as being too elementary or unnecessary for organizational change. As people, we never outgrow stories. Stories disarm people; they connect with the emotional brain that is triggered by change. They also help us understand the problem we are trying to solve and the vision for our future. Storytelling can provide invaluable perspective into why we need to change and what the future can look like. You may be thinking, "Well what if I am not a great storyteller?" You don't have to be; find the people that can help you tell the story for change. You will be surprised how much stories can provide in addition to the facts and numbers. In The book "Switch" by Dan and Chip Heath, they introduce the metaphor of the Elephant and the Rider. The Elephant represents our emotional mind, as our emotions drive us to move. The Rider is our logical mind, which steers our direction. Both of these elements are essential for change. Stories help motivate the Elephant. Can you imagine a Rider sitting atop an Elephant that refuses to move? As a change navigator, the emotional aspect of change cannot be underestimated. People are humans all the time; stories bring people understanding, comfort, and entertainment. If you have a good story, people will be more willing to listen, negotiate, and work with you. Stories will help people to buy you, and that is key for buy-in.

Gaining Buy-In

Have you ever felt that you were leading or involved in a change that people just felt meh about? Were people disinterested in attending meetings, reading communications, or attending training?

I am going to give you a Free tip so you can help prevent that from happening to you. Are you ready?

Fun-Make the change fun; don't make everything you do about the work or project. Celebrate people and wins, have project parties. Do a team escape room or team building, incorporate fun into how you present. Provide free food and music. Create the logo or marketing statement together and let your audience vote on the final options.

Reward-Recognize and show appreciation for people's time and effort. Provide prizes that create positive association with the change. Ensure that new roles or desired behaviors are included in merit reviews and promotion considerations. Don't wait until the end. Change can be a lengthy process and constantly providing reward for small wins helps refuel people for the longer journey,

Excite-Get people excited about change. When you excite people, you generate energy and momentum that get you going in the right direction. When something happens that you are excited about, you often forget about the not so fun work ahead because you are excited for that new element of life. For example, if you have children, think about how excited you were when you first learned you were going to be a parent. If you were excited then you weren't as concerned with all the diapers you were going to change. Or maybe when you got the offer letter for your new job you didn't think about the pain of packing up and moving or saying goodbye to your friends at your old job.

How do you excite people? The simple way is to be exciting! Be creative in how you communicate, be colorful in how you present. People buy you before they buy-in to the change. Coach your sponsor to be an excitable and engaged advocate. Create opportunities to communicate in ways that can relay your excitement.

Engage-Engage people to be a part of the change rather than a target of change. Engage your champions, engage people to be a part of the solution, engage people to voice their questions and concerns and follow up in addressing them.

And one Bonus E. Be E**asy**; don't overcomplicate things. Refrain from jargon or using technical language with nontechnical people. Use layman's terms, analogies, and stories that people can relate to. Remove or eliminate non value added tedious work. Change is hard, so don't make it harder than it needs to be.

People have free will to change or not. If you want people to buy-in, make it Free.

Sponsors and Champions

Who's your favorite Wheaties box athlete? Have you ever gone to YouTube for advice on a decision? If so, you've been introduced to versions of sponsors and champions. These are people you trust or maybe even look up to. Their opinions can be the reason you decide to change or not.

A Change Sponsor is a person typically in a senior position that approves and advocates for a change. Sponsors are key partners for you because they can motivate people to change.

Sponsors also supply resources that can help the project be successful. They can de-prioritize conflicting change efforts that may reduce ability for change and can hold leadership accountable in supporting and reinforcing new behaviors.

For example, imagine your organization rolled out brilliant new software that finally freed you from creating excel charts every

Friday. But then your manager insists you keep doing it the old way; it'll be difficult for you to be successful. Your sponsor should give people confidence that the future will be supported by senior leadership.

Your sponsors should have in-depth knowledge of how the change affects the organization and be visible at major meetings and functions that support the change.

Next are your Change Champions.

Change champions are people who represent the needs, opinions, and views of their teams and functions during the change journey. They provide key insights to the project and change team because they know firsthand how change impacts their perspective areas. They're also key partners and critical liaisons in engaging and supporting the team impacted by change.

As mentioned earlier, Champions are trusted resources for communicating details of change because they know their team's perspective and have empathy for them. By investing time and information in your champions, you empower them to help promote and facilitate change, without more efforts from the project team. It's like investing your money in a high interest account and just watching your account grow.

Who can be a Change Champion? Anyone who's committed to the change and who has the perspective and ability to influence people affected by it. Don't limit your change champion network to senior leaders or managers. Think of how communication happens in your organization; when people have questions their first source is typically their friend at the next desk. They may ask "Hey Nina, what's this about? Do you know anything about this?" People typically don't knock on their boss's office for every question. You need people on the front line to tell you about what is happening on the front lines. It is great to have senior leadership champions also, but don't stop there.

So, when you're preparing your change make sure that you have a sponsor that is invested in and advocating for the change. Coach them to be visible, personable, and as transparent as possible.

Then, build a strong network of Change Champions who represent the departments, roles, sites, regions, and countries of your organization. You can start today by identifying and recruiting these champions and building relationships with them. Don't forget to show them you appreciate them, because you need them.

Embrace Resistance

As a change navigation leader, people often ask me, "Why do people resist change?" My answer is often this: people aren't resisting change; they are challenging change.

What's the difference? To imply that people are resisting change carries the stigma that they are being stubborn or unwilling to move into the future and that the onus to change is merely on them. To challenge change is to gather information about the change, so people can make an informed decision to embrace it or if the change solution needs to be revisited. When change is challenged, the onus is on the change team to supply what people need to make the decision to change. Do not fear resistance; use it as an opportunity to learn, inform, and revisit the solution you are proposing. If you are not comfortable that the change effort can stand up to challenges, it is possible that the problem is not resistance but rather the change you are proposing lacks the value or design necessary to meet sustained adoption.

What you may consider to be resistance may just be the playing out of the natural process of change. People have this reaction because they're uncertain; they have questions. In this lesson I'll walk you through the key questions people have about new change, and how to best handle those questions and concerns so they don't become truly resistant.

The four questions people have about change are:

Why - Why does this matter?

What - What exactly is going to be different?

How - How will this affect them?

And Who - Who's involved?

Let's start with Why?

The reason the change must happen is the most important thing to translate and communicate. By translate I mean to translate the why from the C-Suite to into a why that relates to your audience. People have distinct roles, goals, and priorities within the organization, so you need to communicate Why this is important to your organization in light of their priorities.

Make sure that people understand why now. People may have conflicting priorities, so even if your why is strong, there needs to be something that creates urgency. Find and focus on the urgent problem or need that is being addressed by this change and explain Why this can't wait until next quarter or next budget.

Now, make the "what" clear. What are the impacts on them; what's changing about their job, the organization, their leadership? What are the benefits and opportunities that can come of this? What are my roles and responsibilities? What is Success?

This is important because the "what" is people's second biggest question about change. Answering these questions will be particularly helpful in making sure people feel confident about the upcoming change.

Next, walk them through the "how." How can they change, how does it work, how will they be trained, how their barrier will be removed, how can they be successful, how will you support them? When change is introduced, it makes people uncomfortable, they need to be secure in understanding how they will be successful and how they will gain more than they lose. You will need to understand what barriers stand in the way of lasting change and how to remove them.

Finally, the "who." Introduce your sponsor and engage them to be an active advocate for the change. People want to know who's leading this effort. Show faces of the project team, represent people that are being asked to change with familiar faces that they trust.

When people "resist" it's largely because they're uncertain. They're seeking information to understand what they're losing and gaining, and if this is worth the energy required to change. They want to know that the information they receive to address their uncertainty comes from a reliable, trusted source.

People resist change because it's so much easier to stay the same. It's easier to sit on the porch with a cool iced tea, on a hot summer day watching the overgrown grass than to get up and mow the lawn so you can see the garden.

By clarifying and thoroughly answering these four questions, you give your people the clarity and motivation they need to take the time to mow that lawn.

Change Turbulence

Are you afraid of flying, or do you know anyone who is? Turbulence can be a scary experience for flyers. But did you know that turbulence is highly unlikely to cause a crash? It's rocky, it's uncomfortable, but it is not dangerous. Turbulence is a result of changes in the environment; it serves as a signal to pilots that there is a need to alter the flight path or altitude. Think of people resistance as turbulence; when there is resistance, it teaches us that we need to alter our approach and elevation as navigators. You may need to change your strategy, the way you communicate, or even your solution. But you do not need to panic; resistance does not mean you're failing, it means you have people's attention now so you need to listen, communicate, and navigate.

Making Change Stick

The role of the change navigator isn't to make sure that change is completed. It's to make sure change is successful. Go Live day, launch, grand opening, or whatever the milestone, is not the end. It needs to stick. The new behaviors need to continue in an optimal way.

Think of it this way: If a person makes a resolution to be more organized, theymight buy filing cabinets, watch YouTube videos, hire a specialist, and finally successfully organize their home. But 3 weeks later their place may be a mess, papers everywhere, they can't find anything. What happened? They organized their home but they didn't become more organized. To organize only requires a series of actions, to be organized requires a change in mindset and behavior.

Here is some GLUE to make changes stick.

The "G" is for Goals-Establish what it means to be successful by setting attainable progressive goals. For example, a common mistake people make with New Year's resolutions is they say things like "I want to get in shape," which is not a measurable goal. Or they say I want to work out 5 days a week, which is measurable, but 0 to 5 is a major jump. If that person goes 4 days, they may see it as a failure and their motivation may dip. But what if the goal was 2 days and they went 3? They exceeded their goal! Now 4 days a week seems reasonable. Organizations may set goals like 100% quality or 0 % error rate, which sets them up for failure and does not support sustainability of new behavior.

The "L" is Leadership-Your leadership needs to reinforce the new state. That means compensations, evaluations, and accountability should reward the new behaviors. For example, if your organization just rolled out a new suite of services that can revitalize your sales, but your manager is only tying your bonuses to the floundering old products, why should you focus on the new ones?

What if you finally convinced your teenage son to stop using his phone at the dinner table but then you start answering work emails at the dinner table. Leadership is powerful and your leadership should be an example of the change, not an exception. It is also important that your leadership is aligned on messaging to be shared with your change passengers. One of the greatest barriers to sustainability is confusion. To commit to future behaviors, we need a common understanding of what those behaviors are and how they will continue to be supported and reinforced--which leads us to U.

Next, "U" is Understanding- People need to understand their Roles and Responsibilities, how things work, what to do when they're having difficulty, and who to contact. If you want to be healthier you need to know how to shop, cook, eat, and sleep healthier. You need to know how to resist those urges for New York style pizza or energy drinks in my case.

If you don't ensure that everyone has a thorough understanding they'll revert to what they know or find a work-around, threatening the success of your change. You will also need to understand what success is and what you are aspiring to. What are your immediate, short-term, and long-distance goals? Make them clear and attainable. Then you will need to evaluate.

Finally, "E" is Evaluate- Continue to measure success, shortly after Going Live, three months later, six months later, and so on. Be ready to provide supplemental training, guidance, or communication where necessary. Follow up to assess people's comfort level and opinions of the new environment. Evaluate for the new behaviors when awarding compensation and merits. Share your progress and even your failures. If you do not meet your goals, create action plans to correct. Learn if there are any remining obstacles that could be in the way of results. Keep in mind that after people have committed so much time and effort to this journey with you, they also want to see success.

Finally, Say Thank You and celebrate accomplishments.

Add the GLUE and watch your change stick.

Thank you for traveling with us

Congratulations, you have successfully navigated your way to the end. I hope that now you understand change navigation and are willing to adopt this approach in your life, community, or organization.

If you're looking to learn more, some resources I'd recommend are:

The Association of Change Management Professionals- This organization is a great resource for people who want to learn about the change management profession and connect with other change management practitioners.

"The Cure for Stupidity" by Eric Bailey- This is a terrific book for understanding perspective and context to improve how you solve problems and improve relationships.

"Switch: How to change things when change is hard"-by Chip & Dan Heath - This offers a great look into situational examples of how you make change easier.

Finally, leading change is a wonderfully rewarding opportunity. You get to experience so many human emotions and watch people and organizations grow and evolve. Most importantly you get to meet new people and build great relationships.

Hopefully, you have or will have the opportunity to affect positive change in your organization, community, or personal journey to achieve a purpose that you believe in and are passionate about.

Change will not be easy, and it will not always go smoothly. Sometimes you may even want to throw your hands to the sky in frustration. That too is natural, because you're going through a change process of your own. But if you execute a mindset to navigate over manage, you will see people move from "I can't" to "I did." And you too can say, "I love it when a plan comes together."

Salute and Salut, sayonara and bon voyage.